AF338295

THE RECEIVER

A Story About Remembering Who We Are

CHRISTY SANBORN

ISBN: 978-1-959563-50-1

Maudlin Pond Press
P.O. Box 53
Tybee Island, GA 31328
www.maudlinpond.com

Printed in the United States of America

I dedicate this book to my husband, Mark,
"the man of my dreams."
Thank you for always believing in me;
your unconditional love for me has
inspired me to shine brighter.

To my extraordinary daughter, Leena,
and my bigger then life son, Weston,
for being the two most beautiful gifts
I have ever received.

Most little girls are
taught to give
give a smile
give a hug
give your time

But few little girls
are ever taught how
to receive

How to receive love
How to receive kindness
How to receive help
How to receive joy

When we forget how
to receive
we forget how to stay
open
we forget how to let
love in
When our little hearts
are open,
love flows easily
in and out
like the waves of the
ocean

Receiving is how we fill
ourselves back up
It is how we remember
that we are already
complete

Sometimes, we close
our hearts because it
feels safer
We watch others give
and give until they are
tired so we learn to
do the same

We think love only
moves in one direction
But love is not meant
to be one way

Love is a circle
It gives
and it receives
again and again

mantra

mother: I am love

daughter: I am love

To receive is to trust
To trust is to be open
To be open is to be
alive

Our Mother Earth
shows us how
she receives sunlight
and rain and she
blossoms in beauty

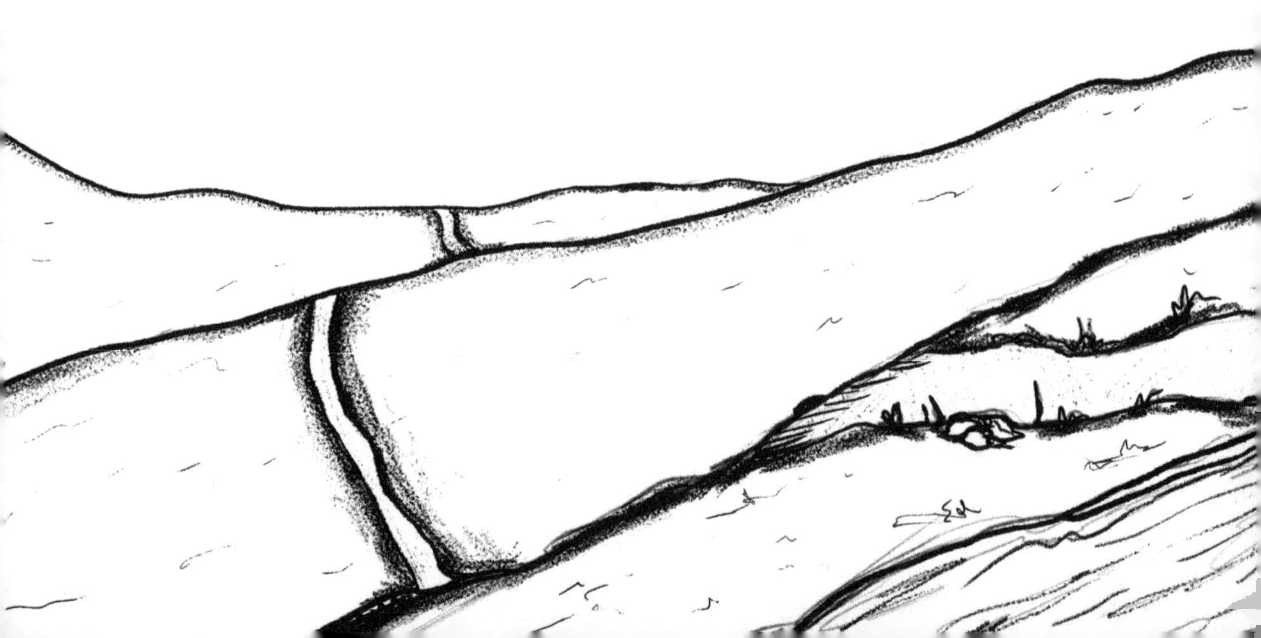

She receives what
she needs and gives
back even more

When we open our
hearts
we remember we are
like her
We are full of love
We are meant to grow
We are connection
We are heart
We are soul
We are divine
We are feminine
We are the receivers

mantra

mother: I am worthy

daughter: I am worthy

When someone gives
you a gift you can
simply smile and say
'Thank you'

You don't have to give
anything back in
return
You don't have
to earn it
You only need
to receive it
and feel worthy of it

Because you are

When someone says,
'You're beautiful'
you can say
'Thank you'
And know it's true

Receiving takes
practice
We can practice filling
our own hearts with
love every day

mantra

mother: my heart is
open

daughter: my heart is
open

When we open,
we trust
When we trust,
we feel safe
When we feel safe,
we blossom

Mother Earth is our
teacher
She is not afraid to
shine
to be seen
to be admired
She gives because
she is full
She receives because
she is open
And through that
giving and receiving
she stays alive and
beautiful

We are just like her
We are meant to grow
to love
to open
to receive
When we block our
hearts, we wither
But when we open
everything blooms

mantra

mother: I am love

daughter: I am love

We are connection
We are heart
We are soul
We are divine
We are feminine
Never forget that

Author Bio

Christy Sanborn is blissfully married and a proud mother of two beautiful children who inspire her to be a better version of herself every day. She lives on the coast of Georgia where she enjoys working as a life coach and radio host.

Christy wrote <u>The Receiver: A Story About Remembering Who We Are</u> for both parents and young girls, with the hope of reminding readers that we all carry a sacred, intuitive wisdom within us. Through this story, she invites readers to reconnect with the divine feminine qualities of presence, intuition, and inner knowing.

Illustrator Bio

Courtney Steele is a Savannah-based, multi-faceted artist who happily follows creativity wherever it decides to wander. From playful illustrations and intuitive abstract color-scape paintings to digital art (and pretty much anything else that sparks her curiosity), she's always exploring new ways to make something interesting.

Above all, Courtney is passionate about chasing her creative ideas wherever they may lead.